LEGACY OF FAITH

Family Edition

JENNIFER M. MORGAN

WESTBOW
PRESS®
A DIVISION OF THOMAS NELSON
& ZONDERVAN

WestBow Press books may be ordered through booksellers or by contacting:

WestBow Press
A Division of Thomas Nelson & Zondervan
1663 Liberty Drive
Bloomington, IN 47403
www.westbowpress.com
844-714-3454

ISBN: 978-1-6642-4990-5 (sc)
ISBN: 978-1-6642-4991-2 (hc)
ISBN: 978-1-6642-4992-9 (e)

Library of Congress Control Number: 2021923222

Print information available on the last page.

WestBow Press rev. date: 12/18/2021

Be strong and courageous, because you
will lead these people to inherit the land I
swore to their forefathers to give them.
Be strong and very courageous. Be careful to
obey all the law my servant Moses gave you; do
not turn from it to the right or to the left, that
you may be successful wherever you go.
—Joshua 1:6-7 (New International Version)

Some miracles are birthed from the smallest seeds of faith in the most impossible circumstances.

This Book is for the

_____

Name

FAMILY LEGACY

_____

Date

Names and Ages

_____

_____

_____

_____

_____

Contents

Foreword... xiii

From the Author xv

What is a Legacy of Faith? xvii

A Note for the Leaders xix

Family Edition xxi

The First Legacy Story 1

The Story.. 3

Just a Little Background.. 4

Creating Your Legacy.. 7

The Letter H 9

Create a Vision 11

Helpful Tips for the Leader... 13

Unexpected Opportunities 15

Conversation Starters 17

Legacy Stones...19

Prayers for Others 43

Bible Promises...48

Living Your Legacy..51

Family Mission Statement.. 54

Our Family Mission Statement 55

When God Says Yes 57

When God Says No 60

When God is Silent.. 63

Surrender Through Prayer 67

Hope.. 70

Rock Collection 73

Prayer Wall 74

Share Your Faith 75

Encouragements for the Journey 85

The Morgans' Favorite Verses 87

God's Yelp Page.. 88

Special Thank You..103

About the Photos.. 107

Notes 109

Resources For Families..111

Other Recommendations to Grow Your Faith.................113

Special Acknowledgments 115

This book is dedicated to my family. May we continue to move forward in faith and fight the good fight so that generations after us will be inspired to do the same.

Bobby, Jordan, and Siara, the "Morgan team," as your dad says, has a great purpose to bring hope to others in a God who saves and redeems. He is full of mercy and always has a good plan. We have definitely seen some tough winters, but we have also seen the seeds that have been planted for a bountiful spring.

As we continue to step into our Jordan Rivers, I pray we will always be bold and courageous. May we always experience God's unconditional love and amazing plan for us as we step into the river and He parts the water right before our eyes.

Foreword

We all have a desire to serve. I've watched Jennifer's desire to serve families grow year after year. Her heart for impacting marriages is profound. I hope that your family gets to really feel that overwhelming love, joy, and hope that she wishes for you to have through this book. May this book truly impact your legacy.

—Bobby

My mom wrote this book because she has the biggest heart to not only see people come to know God, but whole families. I had the privilege of having a ton of "mommy and son" talks over the years with her that have contributed to the person I am today. The one thing that has stuck with me through all the trials we have been through is to never lose your faith. You must keep pushing through. Sometimes you won't see the purpose of your difficulties until much later, just as our family has seen. I continue to hold onto that same faith today.

—Jordan (22)

My mother is very talented, especially when it comes to cleaning the house. She is also a very grateful person. She teaches me to be grateful for what I have and notice that not everyone has the same thing. My mother is probably the most humble person you will ever find. She is so amazing for what she does in this family. She is so wonderful. She is family.

—Siara (9)

From the Author

Who am I? I am just Jen, a stay-at-home mom and a writer of the things God puts on my heart to share. According to my daughter, I also have an amazing talent in house cleaning. I am what I like to consider a home-schooled disciple of Jesus.

I truly believe future generations are in need of our stories. They need to know that God will be with them through their smallest and their toughest circumstances. This book may not be interesting to your younger children right now, but one day, when they are older, they will pick it up to read the stories about how their family saw God in their lives in the good and the bad. They will remember the times you met to talk to them about God.

I hope as you daily live out your legacy and record your stories in this book, that above all you will see how much the creator of the universe loves you and your family. Let this book be a new adventure on your faith journey as you seek to discover all the beautiful facets of the character of God and His loving ways.

What is a Legacy of Faith?

Most people work very hard to leave behind a financial legacy to their children and grandchildren. Have you ever asked yourself how you can impact the next generation by leaving behind a legacy of stories of your faith in God? When we retell our faith stories, they remind us to be strong in our times of weakness. They also remind us of who God is. It is inspiring to hear stories of heroic Bible characters, but what if those stories were about your mom and dad or grandma and grandpa? This book is designed to help your family be intentional about sharing and recording God's involvement in your everyday lives.

While going through this book, you will record the stories of how you are growing in your faith in the same way you would put photos in an album of your family at different stages of their lives. As you begin recording God's activity in your lives and start looking for His responses to your prayers, you and your family will eventually build a deeper relationship with Him and with each other.

A Note for the Leaders

When my family started going through this book together, we all had different ideas of what we wanted our time together to look like. My preteen was hesitant on day one about participating. We did not pressure her to contribute, but only requested that she be present. She slowly came around and even volunteered to lead our meetings a few times. My adult son looked forward to meeting so he could hear more about our daily lives. During the weeks we met, he became more intentional about praying and was really encouraged to see how active God was in his life.

My husband was a huge encouragement whenever I wanted to give up. You will need people in your lives to have faith that is stronger than yours in moments of weakness. I highly recommend finding people to pray for you and your family as you begin to meet.

The week after we committed to going through the book, my husband was offered a unique opportunity to work a temporary job three thousand miles away from home. I really wanted to support him in it, so he took it. I shed a lot of tears trying to get our family devotional time to look the way I thought it should, but eventually I realized I had to remain flexible. At times we had to set up electronic devices to view and chat with each other online. Sometimes, there were some of us who were late or not present. We committed to still meet and accepted that during this season things would be less than ideal. What we did not realize was that God already had a plan to keep us all connected through this book while my husband was away.

If meeting together is not something you do regularly, scheduling time may feel a little messy at first, especially if you are working with the schedules of adult children. Sharing your lives with each other may seem awkward if communications in your home or with your children is not intimate or transparent already. As the leader, just begin to model the expectation, and eventually everyone will follow suit.

All I can say is, do not give up! It may not come together as easily as you hoped in the beginning. The truth is that we have a real enemy who does not want us to spend time with our families, let alone meet to create legacies of faith. You may have to be ready to stand firm and fight until it gets easier. I can guarantee that if you do, the rewards will be some of your best stories. Be strong and courageous, my friends. Be strong and courageous! God is with you, and He wants you to win this battle.

Family Edition

Family, by Jesus's definition was, "For whoever does the will of my Father in heaven is my brother and sister and mother" (Matthew 12:50). Those you invite to be a part of your book will probably be your immediate family, but you can also invite those outside of your family to join you. This can even include people who do not know Jesus. They can participate in some of the conversation starters, but what will be even more exciting is that they will get to listen to your stories of faith.

It's time for us as the church to rise up, to invest and fight for our families. When we build strong, loving families, we become salt and light to the world. We build the church from the inside out.

I hope this book will be a tool for your family to grow closer to God and each other as we invite others to do the same.

The First Legacy Story

The Story

Joshua called out the twelve men whom he selected from the People of Israel, one man from each tribe. Joshua directed them, "Cross to the middle of the Jordan and take your place in front of the Chest of God, your God. Each of you heft a stone to your shoulder, a stone for each of the tribes of the People of Israel, so you'll have something later to mark the occasion. When your children ask you, 'What are these stones to you?' you'll say, 'The flow of the Jordan was stopped in front of the Chest of the Covenant of God as it crossed the Jordan—stopped in its tracks. These stones are a permanent memorial for the People of Israel.'" (Joshua 4:4–7 MSG)

Just a Little Background

Joshua was called by God to take the Israelites into the Promised Land, a flourishing area that was set aside for them. However, they had to confront their enemy and overcome great obstacles in order to take back the land. Moses had previously led the Israelites out of Egypt and across the Red Sea, which God had miraculously parted to deliver them from slavery. However, because they doubted God and complained on the way to the Promised Land, they were not allowed to enter it. They died in the desert over a period of forty years.

Joshua and Caleb had trusted God and were the only ones who'd believed they could conquer their enemies when they were sent to spy on them in the land years before. Along with the children of the previous generation, they became the only ones allowed to enter the Promised Land. Under Joshua's leadership, they moved forward to claim the land promised to them by God.

Crossing the Jordan River was their first step. It was also their first challenge. Joshua and the Israelites did not have their enemies pursuing them like Moses had. They were actually about to enter their enemy's territory to attack them. Before they could do this, they had to cross the Jordan River, which was at flood stage during the harvest. Just like the Red Sea, it needed to be parted so they could walk through it.

God's directions to Moses for crossing the Red Sea were different than the directions He gave to Joshua. God told Moses, "Raise your staff and stretch out your hand over the sea to divide the water so that the Israelites can go through the sea on dry ground" (Exodus 14:16). Joshua, on the other hand, was told, "Tell the priests who carry the Ark of the Covenant: 'When you reach the edge of the Jordan's waters, go and stand in the river'" (Joshua 3:8).

I heard a pastor on the radio point out that Moses was able to see the miracle of the Red Sea parting before they even stepped into it to cross over. Joshua, on the other hand, did not get to see the water part until after he stepped into it. God required that the ark of the covenant be carried into the water first. God made a way only after they obeyed and stepped into the water, driven by nothing more than their faith that God would do what He said He would.

"Then you will know which way to go, since you have never been this way before" (Joshua 3:4). God was leading them differently than He had led the previous generation. They needed to pay attention to God's direction because they would have to do things differently than their parents had done them.

The ark of the covenant and its contents represented some key things that are symbolic to our faith today. The blood of the lamb that was sprinkled upon the ark of the covenant represents what we now have through Jesus, who is our covering of sin. We no longer have to sacrifice animals in order to be forgiven or to speak to God. We can have a close relationship with God because Jesus, His son, died on a cross and was resurrected. He became the last sacrifice for our sins.

The ark of the covenant contained manna, which was a miraculous provision of food they'd received from God when they left Egypt and were crossing the desert. The ark also contained the budding staff that belonged to Aaron, Moses's coleader. Lastly, it had the Ten Commandments, God's list of commands given to Moses for the people to guide them in righteousness. I believe these items were set apart and saved to remind them of God's miraculous provision, His divine choice of leadership, and His desire for the righteousness of His people. The Promised Land was not handed over to the Israelites. They had to fight for it.

Once they crossed the Jordan River, they were told to find twelve stones to set up as a memorial of the miracle God just performed. God wanted their children to ask about the stones one day so that they could retell the amazing story of when He parted the Jordan River for them to cross. This time they would not forget the miracles that God had performed, and it would help them when they had to trust God for future battles.

You may be asking, what does any of this have to do with me today? We are the Joshua generation of today. We are called to move forward in faith-filled victories in all areas of our lives. We may be called to go and do things that no one we know has done before. Sometimes we have to confront big enemies in our lives. Those enemies can be fear, addiction, or a difficult relationship. Whatever it is, God wants us to remember all that He has done so that we can have the faith to believe that He can do it again.

Creating Your Legacy

The Letter H

The printing of the first edition of this book was funded by generous donors as a gift to my daughter's fourth-grade class in 2016. The day had finally arrived! After opening the box and glowing with excitement, I pulled out the brand-new book to admire the shiny, new cover. As I examined the binder, the title read LEGACY OF FAITH. It was all in bold black letters except for the letter *h*! It was the only letter colored in white. Screech! It was like that moment in movies where a record player scratches to a halt in the middle of a harmonious tune. *What?* The printer must have made a mistake, or even worse, maybe it was my mistake? It was so late at night when I sent the finished draft to the printer. I must have missed it!

I was presenting them to the class in a few days, and there was not enough time to reorder them. I had to fix it. After coloring in the *h* on one of the books with a black fine-tip marker, I immediately had a change of heart. I decided to leave the letter just as it was on all the other copies, uncolored and in white. I would use it as an opportunity to teach the students that sometimes we make mistakes, even if we gave it our best.

The day had come for me to present the books. I was given strict instructions to only share about the writing process. I was reminded that it was a public school and I could not share about the faith-based content of the book. After I finished sharing about the letter *h*, a student in the back of the class asked me if I could tell her what the word was that had the mistake. As I smiled, I said, "The word is *faith*."

I originally thought stories similar to David and Goliath or Daniel in the lion's den were the only tales worthy of recording in a book on faith. Those stories are amazing, and David and Daniel are examples of people who had great faith under challenging circumstances, but those stories were not in the Bible to tell us how amazing they were. Those stories were there to reveal God, who was worthy of trust. Our stories of faith are not about *our* greatness but about the greatness of God.

The letter *h* gave me the platform to speak about my mistake and encourage young writers to keep going when they make mistakes. It gave me the opportunity to speak the word "faith" in a public-school classroom where it was forbidden. The letter *h* represents our sins that give us the platform to speak about God's amazing grace and mercy for us. Amazing stories of faith are not meant to shine the light on what we have done, rather our stories of faith are meant to shine the light on who God is and what He has already done.

In case you are wondering, I did not write this book because I have unquenchable faith. I wrote this book while I had doubts of its purpose and my ability to write it. Yes, it took obedience, but it was only because I had come to know a God who takes our simple acts of obedience in the midst of doubt and turns them into stories that reveal who He is. He is a God we can trust, and He invites us to be a part of the bigger story.

Create a Vision

What was the last good story you heard or television show you watched? Did you laugh or cry? Did it make you sit for hours binging on cliffhangers from one to the next? Good stories draw out our emotions, and even better stories impact us to change the way we do things.

Your legacy will be a compilation of your stories of faith as you walk with God through life. Your stories will be the blockbuster favorites in your family. They will be the stories that make the type of impact that will change the lives of those in your family because they will be the real stories about your adventures with God, written by *you*!

Take some time to pray with your family and create a personal vision for your Legacy of Faith book. Ask each member in your family what their hope is for the time you spend together and for the future generations that will read what you record in this book. Your hope may be that one day you want your grandchildren to sit around a table every Thanksgiving reading a different story from the book. You may want your great-great-grandchildren to be inspired by your stories to do things previous generations were too scared to do. Your vision will be the thing that will keep you motivated to continue writing in your book.

Our vision for this book ...

_____

_____

_____

_____

_____

_____

_____

_____

_____

_____

_____

_____

_____

_____

Helpful Tips for the Leader

There is no right or wrong way to go through this book, but below are a few suggestions that might be helpful.

1. Keep it simple. Try not to turn it into a Bible study. The hope is to create an open time of sharing for everyone. Take turns reading through the pages out loud.
2. If you are married, meet with your spouse before you start going through it with your family so you can pray and discuss the format you want to use.
3. Make a special dinner on the days you plan to meet.
4. Use the conversation starters to start off your meeting. Do not force sharing. Ask a lot of questions.
5. Everyone does not have to make an entry in the book every week. Continue to share your own personal God sightings and others will learn to do the same. Family members can share how they see God active in other family member's lives also.
6. Read the previous journal entry the next time you meet to see if there have been any updates or to celebrate and remind everyone of what God did.
7. Elect one writer in the family to put the stories in the book.
8. Write down prayer requests for each person present. Try to focus on personal prayer requests instead of prayers for people who are not there. Ask the question, "How can we pray for you this week?"
9. With discretion, share prayer requests that are real and specific to your current struggles. The more transparent you are as a leader with your personal struggles, the more you will allow your children to know that everyone struggles.

10. Be open to how God will lead the format each time you meet. It may not look the same every week, depending on what is happening in each family member's life.
11. If you have a large family, you can create prayer partners. Take time during your meeting to meet with your prayer partner. and then come together and record the requests after you meet with your partner.
12. Find people outside of your family to pray for you as your family begins to meet. Getting started can sometimes have its challenges. and you will need someone who can be covering you in prayer as you fight to establish this time with your family.
13. Have fun! Talking about what is happening in your lives and how God is working may be new for some family members. Over time, it will get easier as it did for us. We found this book to be a true blessing to our family. Now we hope it will be the same for your family too.

Unexpected Opportunities

Our biggest challenges can be seen as opportunities. Try not to create too many expectations as to how you want your time with your family to go every week. God may have something completely different planned for your meetings.

How do you keep disinterested children engaged?

Sometimes you may just have a season where some of your children may not be interested. Eventually they will open up. If they are too young, then let them color or do something else while you talk with the children who can participate.

How to keep little ones occupied while the family is talking?

Have a neighborhood babysitter sit with your little ones for an hour, so you can have uninterrupted time to talk.

How do you keep non-believing family members from feeling left out?

Start your times out with a casual conversation starter like sharing your "highs and lows" of the week. Share authentically what is going on in your life without the intent of teaching or trying to convert them.

What do you do with family members who are negative or do not want to participate?

I would not pressure anyone to participate. In our situation, we just required our reluctant 12-year-old to be present. You may eventually find that there is a deeper reason behind why they do not want to participate.

How do you deal with chaotic schedules or distance?

Be ready to give grace for those who cannot join every week. Try to keep a consistent day and time. Use digital media. Keep the person updated on what they missed if they could not attend. Let them know they were missed and get their prayer request for the week.

Conversation Starters

- What has been your high (best thing that happened) and low (worst thing that happened) during your week?

- What is something you are praying for this week?

- What happened this week that you did not expect to happen?

- Take turns sharing a positive quality that you believe you have, or share something positive about someone else in the family.

- Ask family members for suggestions on how to add something fun each week to your family time.

- Share an answer to prayer that you saw during your week.

- What is a new tradition you would like to start?

- Do you have a legacy story to record in the book?

- What do you hope future generations will remember about you?

- What is one thing you want to get better at this year?

- What is something you learned from a mistake you made last week?

They triumphed over him
by the blood of the Lamb
and by the word of their testimony;
they did not love their lives so much
as to shrink from death.
—Revelations 12:11

Legacy Stones

The Israelites were told to find twelve stones from the Jordan River. God wanted them to set the stones up as a reminder of the miracle He had performed of parting the Jordan River. The hope was that their children would ask about the stones, and they would one day be able to retell the story of how God provided for them and made a way for them in their time of need.

So what does a legacy stone look like and how do we learn to look for them? A legacy stone is a memorable moment or story of God's presence in your life or circumstances. It can also be a Bible verse that has encouraged you, an answer to prayer, or a person He sent to help you. God's fingerprints in our lives resemble things that only He can do. It could be found in something small like finding a parking space, or in a bigger gesture of saving you from serious health issues.

You may even see Him present when He did not answer your prayer the way you wanted Him to, but He showed up through His comfort and grace. God sometimes reveals Himself in times when we cannot hear Him, feel Him, or see Him, and someone else may need to help us notice that He is there.

One year, my daughter went to summer camp and was looking forward to experiencing God in worship the same way she had previously at winter camp. He didn't reveal Himself in the same way, so she came home disappointed. A few weeks later, she shared a memory about camp with me about how she was walking on a path and ran into a swarm of ladybugs. When I heard this, I excitedly told her that I prayed that God would reveal himself to her in microscopic ways while she was at camp. We also remembered how God used a ladybug on her bedroom window to cheer her up during a difficult time the previous year. I was able to help her connect the dots so she could see that God was there. He just revealed Himself in a different way. The biggest blessing of sharing your journey of faith with others is that sometimes they are able to see and point out God to us in things we may have completely missed.

These pages are for you and your family to fill with your stories of God's activity in your lives so they can be retold for many generations to come.

A new command I give you: Love one another. As I have loved you, so you must love one another.
—John 13:34

Prayers for Others

Jesus tells us to love others as He has loved us, because we can't give away love that we have not received. These pages are for prayer requests and answers to prayer for others in your life.

Therefore, everyone who hears these words
of mine and puts them into practice is like a
wise man who built his house on the rock.
—Matthew 7:24

Bible Promises

List your favorite Bible promise or life verse that you would like to record for future generations.

_____

_____

_____

_____

_____

_____

_____

_____

_____

_____

_____

Living Your Legacy

Where there is no revelation, people cast off restraint;
but blessed is the one who heeds wisdom's instruction.
—Proverbs 29:18

Family Mission Statement

All successful companies have a mission statement. Part of leaving a successful legacy of faith is having a mission statement for your family. Have your family pray and share what they believe God's purpose is for your family. Then put it all together to form your family's mission statement. After attending a parenting class at our church, our family created this mission statement.

United, Creative, Inspiring, Redeemed
"May we be a family, united in Jesus and each other as God
continues to create in us something from nothing through our
stories of overcoming. We pray we can creatively inspire hope
in others through our stories of being redeemed by Him."

I pray your mission statement will inspire your family and give you a unified purpose.

For more ideas go to: Focus on the Family website
Writing A Family Mission Statement
http://www.focusonthefamily.com/parenting/spiritual-growth-for-kids/
writing-a-family-mission-statement

Our Family Mission Statement

_____

_____

_____

_____

_____

_____

_____

_____

_____

_____

_____

_____

_____

But seek first his kingdom and his righteousness,
and all these things will be given to you as well.
—Matthew 6:33

When God Says Yes

And the LORD remembered her. So in the course of time
Hannah became pregnant and gave birth to a son. She named
him Samuel, saying, "Because I asked the LORD for him."
—1 Samuel 1:19–20

Hannah cried out to God because she really wanted to have a child. Her enemy mocked her as she desperately prayed. She vowed that she would dedicate his life to the Lord and never cut his hair.

Hannah's prayer was answered, and she dedicated her son, Samuel, to the Lord. Many people have prayed the prayer Hannah did. 'God, if you do this for me, I will do this for you!'

In Lauren Hillenbrand's book, *Unbroken*, Louie Zamporini, a soldier during World War II, made a deal with God to rescue him because he was stranded in enemy waters on a raft. It wasn't until many years after his miraculous rescue, when he attended a Billy Graham Crusade, he remembered his promise, so he decided to commit his life to serving God.

I don't recommend making deals with God to get what you want. However, I do recommend that if He does answer your prayer, that you would share with others what He has done. Just as the Israelites were encouraged to share their story of faith with their children, I believe we are called to do the same.

There are plenty of stories of favorable answers to prayer where Jesus healed people. God has spared many people's lives. He has also kept people safe and helped them win battles.

Sometimes answers to prayer are brought to fruition through obedience. Jesus told the blind man to wash his eyes in the Pool of Siloam. Another person was told to take up his mat. There is evidence that not only faith was needed, but action based on that faith was required. In one case, a man who needed healing asked for more faith even though he said he believed. Matthew 17:20 speaks about only needing faith as small as a mustard seed to change things that are larger than life.

Most of the time, miracles produced a unique intimate experience for the believer and Jesus. A paralyzed man was lowered through the roof by his friends to meet Jesus. He first tells the man his sins are forgiven because of the faith He saw in his friends. When He saw the people were confused about His authority to forgive sins, Jesus told the man to get up and go home. Jesus did a physical healing to show that He had the power to forgive sins. Sometimes God does miraculous things that we can see so that we will believe that He is able to do other things in His spiritual kingdom.

I wish I could give you a formula for why God chooses to say yes to some prayers and not others, but I cannot. In James 4:2–3, we are told that we "do not have because we do not ask," but then in the next sentence it says that "when we do ask, we do not receive, because we ask with wrong motives." Sometimes, God says no, and we may never understand why.

He answered, "Love the Lord your God with
all your heart and with all your soul and with
all your strength and with all your mind."
—Luke 10:27

When God Says No

2 Samuel 12:16–25

David prayed a lot, and he also fasted. David cried out to God while lying on the ground pleading with Him to spare the life of his son. God referred to David as "the man after His own heart." He surely was not perfect, but David's heart was close to God, and he shared all of his deepest feelings. God desires for us to share our most intimate true feelings with Him, the good, the bad and the ugly.

When David's son died, he went to worship God. It did not change his relationship with God, and his worship reflected an acknowledgement of this. David knew God could have saved his son, and that was why he pleaded in prayer for his life. After his son died, David responded with, "Can I bring him back again?" (2 Samuel 2:23).

We have all prayed for something and got something different than what we prayed for. I think that God wants us to ask and share our deepest longings with Him regardless of how He chooses to answer. We may not understand why God says no, but we do know He is always a good Father.

Sometimes our desire to understand everything makes it challenging to accept God's answer, because He does not always explain why. Some people have left their faith because God didn't answer their prayer the way they wanted Him to answer it. Sometimes people begin to doubt the goodness of God or whether He really exists. A negative answer to prayer can be a real test.

Since the first edition of this book came out, my father-in-law passed away from a short battle with lung cancer. I had a belief that my father-in-law would win his battle with cancer. I could not understand why things went differently. I began to question my ability to hear God and even the power of prayer.

After a time of grieving, I came to believe that God's no was wrapped in mercy for my father-in-law. He was in a lot of pain. As a veteran of war and a retired sheriff, he was very familiar with having to be strong in battle. With his devoted wife, his daughter and son by his side, he was released to sit this one out. It took me some time before I could reconcile my feelings about his death, but I had to realize it was okay for things to not be okay.

I have found that moving on from difficult experiences can mean giving ourselves the opportunity to *not* move on, allowing ourselves to grieve the "no." It can also be a time to acknowledge how we feel about God's answer to our prayers, even if it is not positive. We may not feel like worshipping like David. However, I have always found when I work through my feelings with God, I eventually feel His comfort and peace again.

"And we know that in all things, he works together for the good for those who love him." (Romans 8:28)

For we live by faith, not by sight.
—2 Corinthians 5:7

When God is Silent

He has made everything beautiful in its time.
—Ecclesiastes 3:11

It may seem difficult when we get a negative answer to prayer, but I believe, silence is worse. If you have never sat in a season of silence with God, it may be hard to understand what I am talking about.

Job was a righteous man who suffered unbelievable loss. During Job's time of long suffering, his feelings and questions are expressed in a thirty-four-chapter dialogue with his friends. Then, in the midst of Job's lamenting, God speaks. Why did God wait until thirty-four chapters later to speak? He spoke only after Job cried his heart out and was harassed by his inner turmoil, along with his wife and his friends' critical comments.

At the end of the book, in Job 42:5, Job says, "My ears had heard of you but now my eyes have seen you." Somewhere amongst all of his suffering and the silence, he had an intimate experience with God that takes his revelation of who God is even deeper. He expresses that his previous knowledge of God was based on what he had heard from people.

Has this ever happened to you? Has someone ever told you a story about someone they admired or knew and then one day you actually got to meet them? As a child, I remember seeing the story of how Jesus multiplied the fish and the loaves on a board with pictures made of felt. However, it was not until many years later when He turned my "less than enough" into "more than enough" did I understand how He provides even when it seems impossible. The stories and the pictures became real. He became my Abba Father whom I could call on in my time of need.

When God is silent in my storm, I have screamed in my pillow. I have exhausted myself while I anxiously awaited the season to end. Eventually it does, and I usually find that even though God was silent, He was always there.

There have been many theories over what Jesus meant when He cried out on the cross, *"Eli, Eli lama sabachthani,"* which in Hebrew means, "My God, my God, why have you forsaken me?" Some think that God couldn't be present because of the sin Jesus was carrying on the cross. My guess is different. I am not a graduate of seminary, but I have come to understand glimpses of the love of God through my times of pain and isolation. I believe God never left Jesus. However, it's possible that because Jesus suffered as a human did, that the pain that He experienced was so physically and emotionally excruciating that it felt as if God were not there.

Have you ever experienced so much pain that it felt like God was not there? Have you ever cried out, "God, where are you?" "Why can't I hear or feel you?" Some people reasoned that God left him because He could not watch His son suffer. I find it hard to believe God left His son in His greatest time of need. Can you imagine leaving your child at their greatest time of suffering?

In Hebrews 2:18, it says, "Because he himself suffered when he was tempted, he is able to help those who are being tempted." Jesus's mission consisted of undergoing human suffering and temptation, so that He could show us that He could relate to our temptations and suffering. He experienced the physical side to suffering as well as the emotional. Feeling abandoned and alone in times of suffering is something many people feel.

In some recent findings of the late Mother Theresa's confidential letters to a priest, it was found that this devoted woman of God had a long period of silence where she did not hear God or feel His presence. Mother Theresa was a devoted Christ follower who helped the poorest of the poor. Why did God leave her? Or did He?

We cannot base our faith on what we can feel or understand. When God is silent, it is good to place ourselves around other people who can remind us of God's truth. It can be a very lonely place, especially if you believe God has abandoned you because of something you did wrong.

I believe we are called to just keep moving forward in faith, just as Mother Theresa did. We can never earn His love or His presence. We can only believe that what He said is true when He says "…And surely I am with you always, to the very end of the age." (Matthew 28:20)

God's silence can also be a signal for us to slow down and put our "listening" ears on. There was a time in my life when I was crying out to God for direction. I had to make some really important decisions, and I could not hear God. Every day I would start my morning off on my patio with my Bible, searching for wisdom and direction. I was an emotional bubble that was about to pop. My deadline to make a decision was approaching. One day, in exasperation, I cried out to God with everything I had. Then God reminded me in the middle of my storm that He had already given me the direction I was looking for. I had put His previous direction aside, because I was too scared to follow it.

The best way for me to describe what could possibly have happened to me is through this story of when my daughter was a baby. We went to rinse off in the shower after a swim in our pool. As soon as I turned on the shower, she began to scream and grabbed tightly onto me. As I tried to calm her down, her cries only became louder. I was the last person she could hear above the shower and her own piercing screams. She could no longer hear me trying to comfort her and tell her that it was only water. Sometimes, we cannot hear God because we are too scared to listen.

So how do you learn to listen when you are scared? As we get to know God as a good Father, we also get to see that even though we may not always like what He says or feel comfortable with where He leads us, He is always doing things for our good.

I have found that building trust with God is like building trust in most relationships. When you build trust in human relationships you spend time with the person and watch how they do things. You may read about them or hear stories from others. Eventually, you get to know them and trust begins to build. When we read the Bible and hear stories about God from others, we begin to trust Him. We also see how He shows up in our relationship with Him even when He is silent. We learn that trusting God is not based on Him doing what we want Him to do; trusting God is based on who He is, and that never changes.

Trust in the Lord with all your heart
and lean not on your own understanding.
In all your ways acknowledge Him and
He will make your paths straight.
—Proverbs 3:5-6

Surrender Through Prayer

Father, if you are willing, take this cup from me;
yet not my will, but yours be done.
—Luke 22:42

Have you ever been skydiving? I have! Your first step out of the plane is your only step out of the plane. True surrender looks like that step. As we observe Jesus in the Garden of Gethsemane, we see Him crying out to His father before He is about to suffer an excruciating death,

Jesus's most human, yet grace-ordained prayer in the Bible is at the point of asking his Father to keep Him from pain. While experiencing great fear of what He would suffer, He willingly surrendered to His Father's plan. I can imagine God's heart was ripping in two as His son cried out for His Father to spare him from the pain. I am sure it was not easy to watch His son suffer at the hands of sinful men, even though He knew it was for a greater purpose. I think sometimes we forget that God has feelings.

There have been things we have had to let our children go through that were painful for them, like growing pains and natural consequences from poor decisions. Sometimes as we release them into the world, by no fault of their own, they suffer innocently at the hands of others. God knows that the things He allows us to suffer can be worked together for our good, but it can also be used for the good of others. Whenever I have suffered through something, I always have a newfound empathy for others who are suffering through the same thing. I have also experienced the kindness and mercy of God, as I have seen others sacrifice their comfort for me. True surrender requires giving up our comfort for the benefit of others just like Jesus did for us.

Sometimes we surrender as a testing or strengthening of our faith. In

Genesis, when Abraham was asked to sacrifice his son Isaac, it revealed to Abraham that he was able to trust God with losing the very thing through which God would fulfill His promise. For those who don't know the story, here is a spoiler alert. God commanded Abraham to stop right before Abraham was going to kill his only son as a sacrifice. God was testing Abraham to see if he would hold anything back from Him, including the son who would bring numerous promised descendants to him for many generations to come. Abraham passed the test.

Surrender can be the toughest place to get to, but once you do, you can experience extraordinary peace. I think it begins with being really honest with God about how you feel. I can remember begging God for answers to my prayers during difficult times. It was only after many nights of pleading that I found myself releasing what I was asking for into God's hands and will. Surrender came through my exhaustion. I would love to say that every time I surrender something that I never try to repossess it. I have had to learn to surrender daily sometimes until I realize that what I am holding onto sometimes creates even more pain than letting it go.

Now faith is confidence in what we hope for
and assurance about what we do not see.
—Hebrews 11:1

Hope

Hope deferred makes the heart sick, but a
longing fulfilled is a tree of life.
—Proverbs 13:12

Have you ever held onto a promise that you read in God's word and it was yet to unfold? I have heard many single women say they longed to be married and have a family. I have also seen married people believing for a miracle in their relationships or with their children. Sometimes these longings hurt so deeply that we feel like we will never be happy without them. Sometimes these longings just make us sick.

The word hope can be used in differing degrees, like the word love. We hope the surgery goes well. We hope we can pay the bills next month. My daughter hoped at one time she could have a pet horse. Are you following me? Sometimes we lose hope because we are hoping in the wrong things. We hope for our personal desires, not necessarily God's will, based on His truth.

In Psalm 37:4 it says, "Take delight in the LORD, and He will give you the desires of your heart." I have found that when I take delight in God, He does give me the true desires of my heart, which are not always the tangible thing I want, but the heart thing behind what I want. Most of us are looking for the things our heart may be lacking like love, acceptance, and respect. These are all things God can give us. Sometimes He does it through things or people, but sometimes it is fulfilled through a direct relationship with Him.

I am sure Moses hoped he would see the Promised Land along with all the thousands of others that crossed the Red Sea with him. However, he never did. Ultimately, he hoped for God's will and plan and that was exactly what unfolded.

When this book was gifted to my daughter's fourth grade class, I had hoped to give the book to all thirty-six students, but because only ten children brought back the school's mandatory permission slip to request the book, that was all I was able to deliver. My hope was that all thirty-six students would take the book home. Was it wrong to hope for this? Of course not. However, God never told me the goal was for every child to take the book home.

As I was sitting in church watching baptisms the day before Christmas Eve, I recognized a woman stepping into the pool. It was the mother of a girl from the school who had received one of my books nearly three years ago! God had a desire to reach this one family, and I got front row seats to watch. Maybe this one mom was His goal? Sometimes we get to see that He truly does care about that "one" family, that "one" girl, that "one" school. "Believe in the Lord Jesus, and you will be saved—you and your household" (Acts 16:31). Clearly the faith of one new believer can have such an impact on those watching. It can save a whole household. When Jesus visited or healed one person, it almost always had an impact on those closest to them or those who lived in their town.

Are you that one believer or that one family that will give others hope because you believed? Hoping in the word of God is hoping in truth. This is the truth that we are called to hold onto. This is the hope I believe that will never fail.

Great is the LORD and most worthy of
praise; his greatness no one can fathom.
One generation commends your works to
another; they will tell of your mighty acts.
They will speak of the glorious splendor of your
majesty, and I will meditate on your wonderful works.
—Psalm 145:3-5

Rock Collection

The Israelites were asked to place stones from the Jordan River in plain view for their children to see as a memorial. Now, I challenge you to do something similar. Find a vase or a bowl, preferably one that is made of glass or that you can see through. Whenever someone in the family sees God move significantly in their life, they can find a rock and place it into the vase. Write a date on the rock and a word that reminds you of what God did.

The goal is to put the vase in a place in your home where visitors will see it and hopefully ask about it. It will definitely be a great reminder to you and your children of all the ways God has moved in your lives.

Prayer Wall

Create a prayer wall in your home. When my daughter was little, she drew a huge tree on construction paper and cut it out. We placed ours on the wall in the hallway. We cut out branches and leaves, and on each leaf we put our prayer requests.

You can also do something simpler like putting Post-It notes with your prayer requests on your fridge or mirror at home. The point is to make the requests visual so that you can remember to pray. Be as creative as you would like, and have fun with it!

Share Your Faith

It is time to share some answers to pieces of your faith story. You can go through these by answering them one at a time during your weekly meetings, or you can fill this out in your own time. You will be amazed at how many things you find that you have not shared with your family before.

1. How and when did you come to know Jesus?
Name:
Age:

2. What is the biggest thing for which you have had to trust God?

3. What scripture has helped you most in your life and why?

4. Which scripture have you struggled with following the most and why?

5. Did you ever wander from your faith? If so, tell the story of how you returned.

6. What gifts do you believe God has equipped you with?

7. Tell about a time God asked you to do something that required great faith in Him.

8. What is your favorite place to meet God and why?

9. What is your favorite story in the Bible and why?

10. What is one quality about God that you really want me to know about?

11. How do you find comfort in God when you are scared?

12. How do you seek wisdom from God?

Share Your Faith (duplicate)

1. How and when did you come to know Jesus?

Name:

Age:

2. What is the biggest thing for which you have had to trust God?

3. What scripture has helped you most in your life and why?

4. Which scripture have you struggled with following the most and why?

5. Did you ever wander from your faith? If so, tell the story of how you returned.

6. What gifts do you believe God has equipped you with?

7. Tell about a time God asked you to do something that required great faith in Him.

8. What is your favorite place to meet God and why?

9. What is your favorite story in the Bible and why?

10. What is one quality about God that you really want me to know about?

11. How do you find comfort in God when you are scared?

12. How do you seek wisdom from God?

Encouragements for the Journey

The Morgans' Favorite Verses

Redemption

I will bring Judah and Israel back from captivity and will rebuild them as they were before. (Jeremiah 33:7)

—Bobby

Strength

I can do all this through him who gives me strength. (Philippians 4:13)

—Jen

Love and Faith

Let love and faithfulness never leave you; bind them around your neck, write them on the tablet of your heart. (Proverbs 3:3)

—Jordan

Hope

For I know the plans I have for you, declares the Lord, plans to prosper you and not to harm you, plans to give you a hope and a future. (Jeremiah 29:11)

—Siara

God's Yelp Page

The following verses came from good friends and family I am honored to know. The words above the verse describe how the verse encouraged them.

Abundant Life

The thief comes only to steal and kill and destroy; I have come that they may have life, and have it to the full. (John 10:10)

—Vivian

Acceptance and Trust

The Lord gave and the Lord has taken away; may the name of the Lord be praised. (Job 1:21)

—Heather S.

All Things Work Together

And we know that in all things God works for the good of those who love him, who have been called according to his purpose. (Romans 8:28)

—Tammy

Assurance

Now faith is confidence in what we hope for and assurance about what we do not see. (Hebrews 11:1)

—Shelly and Jay

Challenging

Love is patient, love is kind. It does not envy, it does not boast, it is not proud. It does not dishonor others, it is not self-seeking, it is not easily angered, it keeps no record of wrongs. Love does not delight in evil but rejoices with the truth. It always protects, always trusts, always hopes, always perseveres. Love never fails. (1 Corinthians 13:4-8)

Clarity

He has shown you, O mortal, what is good.
And what does the Lord require of you?
To act justly and to love mercy
and to walk humbly with your God. (Micah 6:8)

—Debbie

Comfort

I lift up my eyes to the mountains—where does my help come from? My help comes from the LORD, the Maker of heaven and earth. He will not let your foot slip—he who watches over you will not slumber; indeed, he who watches over Israel will neither slumber nor sleep. The LORD watches over you the LORD is your shade at your right hand; the sun will not harm you by day, nor the moon by night. The LORD will keep you from all harm—he will watch over your life; the LORD will watch over your coming and going both now and forevermore. (Psalm 121)

—Jacque

Comfort

In righteousness you will be established:
Tyranny will be far from you; you will have nothing to fear.
Terror will be far removed; it will not come near you.
If anyone does attack you, it will not be my doing;
whoever attacks you will surrender to you.
"See, it is I who created the blacksmith who fans the coals into flame and forges a weapon fit for its work.
And it is I who have created the destroyer to wreak havoc;
no weapon forged against you will prevail, and you will refute every tongue that accuses you. This is the heritage of the servants of the Lord, and this is their vindication from me." (Isaiah 54:14–17)

Comfort

For I know the plans I have for you," declares the Lord, "plans to prosper you and not to harm you, plans to give you hope and a future. (Jeremiah 29:11)

—Sherry

Confidence

Trust in the Lord with all your heart and lean not on your own understanding; in all your ways submit to him, and he will make your paths straight. (Proverbs 3:5–6)

—Joya

Confidence

I can do all things through him who gives me strength. (Philippians 4:13)

—Baldwin

Connecting Power

The Spirit of the Lord is on me, because he has anointed me to proclaim good news to the poor. He has sent me to proclaim freedom for the prisoners and recovery of sight for the blind, to set the oppressed free. (Luke 4:18)

—Dale

Courage

But Jesus immediately said to them: "Take courage! It is I. Don't be afraid." (Matthew 14:27)

—Rosie

Courage

God is within her, she will not fall; God will help her at break of day. (Psalm 46:5)

—Emily

Destiny

For I know the plans I have for you," declares the Lord, "plans to prosper you and not to harm you, plans to give you hope and a future. (Jeremiah 29:11)

—Jeff

Empathy

Jesus wept. (John 11:35)

—Michael

Eternal Life

For God so loved the world that he gave his one and only Son, that whoever believes in Him shall not perish but have eternal life. (John 3:16)

—Lydia

Faith Above All

For we live by faith, not by sight. (2 Corinthians 5:7)

—Selena

Faithful

The Lord will guide you always; he will satisfy your needs in a sun-scorched land and will strengthen your frame. You will be like a well-watered garden, like a spring whose waters never fail. (Isaiah 58:11)

—Jessica

Flawed

Do not judge, and you will not be judged. Do not condemn and you will not be condemned. Forgive, and you will be forgiven. (Luke 6:37)

—Steve

Freedom

You, my brothers and sisters, were called to be free. But do not use your freedom to indulge the flesh; rather, serve one another humbly in love. (Galatians 5:13)

—Cassie

God's Greatness

Who has measured the waters in the hollow of His hand, Or with the breadth of His hand, marked off the heavens? Who has held the dust of the earth in a basket, Or weighed the mountains on the scales and the hills in a balance? Who has understood the mind of the Lord, or instructed Him as his counselor? Whom did the Lord consult to enlighten Him, and who taught Him the right way? Who was it that taught Him knowledge or showed him the path of understanding? (Isaiah 40:12–14)

—Karen L.

God's Laws

For Ezra had devoted himself to the study and observance of the Law of the Lord, and to teaching its decrees and laws in Israel. (Ezra 7:10)

—Charlotte

God's Word

For the word of God is alive and active. Sharper than any double-edged sword, it penetrates even to dividing soul and spirit, joints and marrow; it judges the thoughts and attitudes of the heart. (Hebrews 4:12)

—Georgia

Grace

But the fruit of the Spirit is love, joy, peace, forbearance, kindness, goodness, faithfulness, gentleness and self-control. Against such things there is no law. (Galatians 5:22–23)

—Sandy

Hope and Encouragement

Is anything too hard for the Lord? I will return to you at the appointed time next year, and Sarah will have a son. (Genesis 18:14)

—Kathy

Hope, Comfort, and Courage

I lift up my eyes to the hills
Where does my help come from?
My help comes from the Lord, the Maker of heaven and earth.
He will not let your foot slip—
He who watches over you will not slumber.
Indeed He who watches over Israel will neither slumber nor sleep.
The Lord watches over you—
The Lord is your shade at your right hand.
The sun will not harm you by day, nor the moon by night.
The Lord will keep you from all harm—
He will watch over your life;
The Lord will watch over your coming and going both now and forevermore.
(Psalm 121)

—Dee

Hope

Instead, they were longing for a better country—a heavenly one. Therefore, God is not ashamed to be called their God, for he has prepared a city for them. (Hebrews 11:16)

—Barb

Humility

Or do you show contempt for the riches of his kindness, forbearance and patience, not realizing that God's kindness is intended to lead you to repentance? (Romans 2:4)

—Faith

Identity

For we are God's handiwork, created in Christ Jesus to do good works, which God prepared in advance for us to do. (Ephesians 2:10)

—Sam

Joy

Rejoice in the Lord always. I will say it again: Rejoice! (Philippians 4:4)

—Kathleen

Justice

Woe to those who call evil good and good evil,
Who put darkness for light and light for darkness,
Who put bitter for sweet and sweet for bitter.
Woe to those who are wise in their own eyes
And clever in their own sight. (Isaiah 5:20-21)

—Stacie

Justice

At that time I will deal with all who oppressed you; I will rescue the lame and gather those who have been scattered. I will give them praise and honor in every land where they were put to shame. At that time I will gather you; at that time I will bring you home. I will give you honor and praise among all the peoples of the earth when I restore your fortunes before your very eyes, says the Lord. (Zephaniah 3:19-20)

Kindness

Anxiety weighs down the heart, but a kind word cheers it up. (Proverbs 12:25)

—Pam

Known

You have searched me, LORD, and you know me. (Psalm 139:1)

—Olivia

Love

And now these three remain: faith, hope and love. But the greatest of these is love. (1 Corinthians 13.13)

—Shaya

My Daily Prayer

Search me, God, and know my heart; test me and know my anxious thoughts. See if there is any offensive way in me, and lead me in the way everlasting. (Psalm 139:23–24)

—LaRosa

Not Alone

No one will be able to stand against you all the days of your life. As I was with Moses, so I will be with you; I will never leave you nor forsake you. (Joshua 1:5)

—Paty

Obedience

Everyone who is committed to the truth hears my voice. (John 18:37)

—Mom

Obedience is Freedom

But the fruit of the Spirit is love, joy, peace, forbearance, kindness, goodness, faithfulness, gentleness and self-control. Against such things there is no law. (Galatians 5:22–23)

—Carlito and Elizabeth

Overcome

Take delight in the Lord and He will give you the desires of your heart. (Psalm 37:4)

—Melani

Overwhelmed

The Lord is my rock, my fortress and my deliverer; my God is my rock, in whom I take refuge, my shield and the horn of my salvation, my stronghold. (Psalm 18:2).

—Monique

Passion

But if I say, "I will not mention his word or speak anymore in his name," his word is in my heart like a fire, a fire shut up in my bones. I am weary of holding it in; indeed, I cannot. (Jeremiah 20:9)

—Epi

Peace

God is within her, she will not fall; God will help her at break of day. (Psalm 46:5)

—Marilyn

Perseverance

For though the righteous fall seven times, they rise again,
but the wicked stumble when calamity strikes. (Proverbs 24:16)

—Dad

Power of Purpose

Many are the plans in a person's heart, but it is the Lord's purpose that prevails. (Proverbs 19:21)

—Heather M.

Pray

Pray continually. (1 Thessalonians 5:17)

—Julie

Promise

The Lord will vindicate me; Your love, Lord, endures forever—do not abandon the works of your hands. (Psalm 138:8)

—Susan

Promise

Here I am! I stand at the door and knock. If anyone hears my voice and opens the door, I will come in and eat with that person, and they with me. (Revelations 3:20)

—Vivian W.

Rejoice, Pray, Thank

Rejoice always, pray continually, give thanks in all circumstances; for this is God's will for you in Christ Jesus. (1 Thessalonians 5:16–18)

—Theresa

Rest

Come to me, all you who are weary and burdened, and I will give you rest. Take my yoke upon you and learn from me, for I am gentle and humble in heart, and you will find rest for your souls. For my yoke is easy and my burden is light. (Matthew 11:28–30)

—Erica

Salvation Accomplished

When he had received the drink, Jesus said, "It is finished." With that, he bowed his head and gave up his spirit. (John 19:30)

—Jane

Sees Me

She gave this name to the Lord who spoke to her: "You are the God who sees me," for she said, "I have now seen the One who sees me." (Genesis 16:13)

—Betty

Stay Prayerful

Be joyful in hope, patient in affliction, faithful in prayer. (Romans 12:12)

—Gina

Strength

I can do all things through him who gives me strength. (Philippians 4:13)

—Fran

Strength

But those who hope in the Lord will renew their strength. They will soar on wings like eagles; they will run and not grow weary; they will walk and not be faint. (Isaiah 40:31)

—Esther

Strength

He says, "Be still, and know that I am God;
I will be exalted among the nations,
I will be exalted in the earth." (Psalm 46:1)

—Denise

Trust

For I know the plans I have for you," declares the Lord, "plans to prosper you and not to harm you, plans to give you hope and a future. (Jeremiah 29:11)

—Bria

Trust

Trust in the Lord with all your heart and lean not on your own understanding. In all your ways acknowledge Him and He will make your paths straight. (Proverbs 3:5–6)

—Barry

Trust

The Lord will fight for you; you need only to be still. (Exodus 14:14)

—Tami R.

Walks With Me

When you pass through the waters, I will be with you; and when you pass through the rivers, they will not sweep over you. When you walk through the fire, you will not be burned; the flames will not set you ablaze. (Isaiah 43:2)

—Cheryl

Wandering

Jesus answered, "I am the way and the truth and the life. No one comes to the Father except through me." (John 14:6)

—Imelda

Wisdom

The law of the Lord is perfect, refreshing the soul.
The statutes of the Lord are trustworthy, making wise the simple. (Psalm 19:7)

—Nate

Work Approved

Do your best to present yourself to God as one approved, a worker who does not need to be ashamed and who correctly handles the word of truth. (2 Timothy 2:15)

—Korey W.

"But by the grace of God I am what I am, and his grace to me was not without effect, No I worked harder than all of them-yet not I, but the grace of God that was with me" (1 Corinthians 15:10).

I found this verse tattooed to a man's arm working in a fragrance store. He shared his story with my husband and I of how he was homeless at one time, and this verse summed up what He saw God do in his life. It basically sums up what He has done in all of our lives and the lives of those who have shared these verses.

Special Thank You

God, to whom all things are made possible, including this book, thank you for your amazing grace "that saved a wretch like me."[1] I am so grateful that you chose us to share your heart's desire for families.

Bobby, my husband, best friend, producer, director, and editor, thank you for helping me bring this book project to life and reading endless pieces of my writing. Thank you for seeing and believing in the gift God has given me even before I saw it. This is a piece of our legacy and I am glad you chose to be a part of it. You are our family's leader of leaders! I will never forget how you loved me when I didn't deserve it. Your story of overcoming will be a legacy that will live on.

Jordan, your gift of compassion for people is contagious. I'm in awe of the leader God is molding you to be. Thanks for your help in publicizing this project. I couldn't have done this alone.

Siara, you grow more and more into the beautiful woman of God He has created you to be. Your courage to stay in difficult situations while standing firm in your beliefs inspires me beyond measure and gives me courage I don't always have. The first edition of this book was inspired by your courage

Mom and Dad, thank you for leaving a legacy of your commitment to your faith and family.

Susan, Mel, and Fran, thank you for loving me like one of your own.

---

[1] *Amazing Grace* lyrics by John Newton

In loving memory of my father-in-law, Robert Morgan, who taught me to have grace for myself during a difficult season. 1946–2016

Family and friends, you have loved and supported me through it all. I wish I had enough room to mention each name and speak of all the love and support, but I would need to write a separate book for all of that. I will never forget you or the blessing you have been to me.

Kathleen, Heather, Vivian, and Karen, thank you for being more than just a friend, but my Simon of Cyrene.

Lydia, Barb, Phylicia, and Paty, God brought each of you at just the right times to encourage me to be a better wife, mom, writer, and to just keep swimming. Thank you.

Tina, Margaret, and Jenny, thank you for encouraging my writing and inviting me to write for your blog to spread my wings and gain some confidence in the gift God has given me. I was truly humbled by the opportunity.

The Keflas, the Morenos, the Tates, the Vegas, and the Winters, thank you for choosing to be the first families I led through the Legacy of Faith book. You are all part of the story now!

Those who contributed to writings, thank you for sharing your life and testimonies that God's word really is living and true. I am blessed to have you in my life

Those who contributed financially, thank you for your investment in the beginning project that propelled this book into existence and gave this book wings to fly.

Jordan Stempson, thank you for the gift of your artwork in the first edition of this book. I will never forget your generosity and patience.

Thank you to all the prayer warriors who have been with me on this writing journey, even those who have joined during the last leg of the race for this book.

Thank you to our many Life groups and family friends that supported and loved on our family, godly men who have been my husband's tribe and people that believed in our marriage and callings when we were weak. This book is a celebration of group faith.

Thank you to my daughter and her special fourth grade class that inspired me to literally "focus up" and finish the first edition of this book in 2016!

About the Photos

The cover photo for this book was taken on the way home from Fremont, California, in 2016. We were headed back from taking my son to his first day of work and getting him settled into his new job 300 miles away from home. He took a job that he had very little experience in and moved into a city where he did not know anyone. His adventure captured a snapshot of the faith that Joshua represents to us. I just knew it had to be the cover photo for the new family edition of this book.

The mystery feet on the back of the book belong to my husband and I. We took this picture in September of 2018, the weekend before he took a temporary job three thousand miles away. It was also the week before we started going through this devotional as a family from beginning to end. Both pictures are snapshots of times that required great faith in unknown circumstances. God was so faithful.

Notes

Living Your Legacy

1   Sheila Seifert and Jeanne Gowen Dennis "WritingFamilyMissionStatement": http://www.focusonthefamily.com/parenting/spiritual-growth-for-kids/writing-a-family-mission-statement.
2   Laura Hillenbrand, *Unbroken* (New York: Random House LLC, 1999), 382.
3   David Van Biema, Mother Theresa's Crisis of Faith
    http://www.time.com.

Encouragement for the Journey

Jehoshua
Strong's Hebrew:
//Hebrew/3091.htm-6k
Iesous
Greek:
//strongnumbers.com/greek2/2424.htm-7k
http://Biblehub.com

All scripture taken from NIV version of the Bible unless otherwise noted.

Resources For Families

These are organizations and books I recommend that help with marriage and family relationships.

Relationship Lifeline

www.RelationshipLifeline.org
For more information, please contact Margaret Aubin:
C 949-698-0868 O 800-718-4650

Relationship 180

Turning relationships in the right direction.
Mission Viejo, CA

How We Love, Milan and Kay Yerkovich
How We Love Our Kids, Milan and Kay Yerkovich

The Five Love Languages, Gary Chapman
The Five Love Languages of Children, Gary Chapman, PhD and Ross Campbell, MD

You and Me Forever, Francis Chan and Lisa Chan

Other Recommendations to Grow Your Faith

Rooted
Kenton Beshore

Breathless
Real Stories of God's Miraculous Power
Stephen P. Campodonico

Portrait of a Woman and Jesus
He looks through Your Eyes and Into Your Heart
Barbara Quillen Egbert

Dinner with Skeptics
Defending God in a World That Makes No Sense
Jeff Vines

The Sabbath Experiment
Spiritual Formation for Living in a Non-Stop World
Rob Muthiah

Special Acknowledgments

These churches and organizations are part of my faith journey and have helped me grow in my relationship with God since I was young. I am grateful for each one of them.

St. Frances of Rome Catholic Church and School, Azusa, CA
Bishop Amat Memorial High School, La Puente, CA
North Orange Christian Church, Orange, CA
107.9 KWAVE radio station
Moms in Prayer International
Christ Church of the Valley, San Dimas, CA
Forest Home Camp, Forest Falls, CA
Brooklyn Tabernacle Church Brooklyn, N.Y.
Saddleback Church. Lake Forest, CA
Mariners Church, Irvine, CA
Hrock, Pasadena, CA
Pasadena International House of Prayer, Pasadena, CA
Lake Avenue Church Women's Bible Study, Pasadena, CA
Fellowship Monrovia, Monrovia, CA
Azusa Pacific University, Azusa, CA

Thank you to just a few of the authors who have unknowingly walked alongside me and inspired me on my spiritual journey: Mark Batterson, Henry and Richard Blackaby, Frances Chan, Catherine Martin, Joyce Meyers, Beth Moore, Stormie Omartian, Francine Rivers, Joanna Weaver, and Sarah Young.

But if serving the Lord seems undesirable to you, then choose for yourselves this day whom you will serve, whether the gods your ancestors served beyond the Euphrates, or the gods of the Amorites, in whose land you are living. But as for me and my household, we will serve the Lord.

—Joshua 24:15

Joshua
Yehoshua
"The Lord is salvation."
Iésous
Jesus

Printed in the United States
by Baker & Taylor Publisher Services